ROSA PARKS

The Woman Who Ignited a Movement

Copyright © 2017 by Hourly History

All rights reserved.

Table of Contents

Introduction
A Dark Legacy
The Winds of Change
The Stage Is Set
The Civil Rights Movement
Life after the Boycott
Conclusion

Introduction

The dark history of slavery came to an end in the United States when the Civil War ended in May of 1865, but the fight for civil rights had only just begun. The U.S. Civil War began when the southern states seceded from the union and formed the Confederate States of America. The uncompromising differences, with regard to the issue of slavery, between the north and the south had prompted this action, but the 16th President of the United States, Abraham Lincoln, refused to recognize the secession. War soon followed, beginning on April 12, 1861, when Confederate soldiers attacked Fort Sumter in South Carolina.

Following the start of the war, President Lincoln signed the Emancipation Proclamation, which freed all slaves, in September of 1862. After nearly three years of bloody conflict, the war ended less than a month following the assassination of Lincoln, who was killed while watching a play at Ford's Theatre in April of 1865. At considerable cost, the northern states prevailed, and slavery became illegal, but the bitterness that characterized the fighting still remains in many parts of the southern U.S. today, and the legacy of slavery still plagues many African-American communities.

Following the Civil War, African-Americans were freed from slavery. Still, they were subjected to horrific discrimination, particularly after the post-war reconstruction period came to an end in 1877. Through the years, the institutional subjugation of African-Americans intensified. Segregation was common and the concept of "separate, but equal" guided much of the legislative process, particularly in the south. Violence against African-Americans was also commonplace, often instigated by militia groups such as the Ku Klux Klan, which had formed as resistance re-emerged.

By the time World War II ended, widespread institutionalized racism had resulted in laws preventing interracial marriage, laws mandating separate public facilities for African-Americans up to and including separate drinking water fountains and bathrooms, and laws preventing African-Americans from attending the same schools, including universities, as European-Americans. This led to the underfunding of African-American facilities, and that subsequently resulted in inferior service. Additionally, prejudice prevented African-Americans from getting well-paying jobs. These policies caused widespread poverty in African-American communities, and furthermore, they made it all but impossible for those trapped in the cycle of poverty to escape.

After participating in World War II to defeat Adolf Hitler, tensions began to build in the United States over its own civil rights record. Hitler's policies exemplified the extremes to which discriminatory practices could be taken, something the United States decried as evil, and yet, America had its own dismal civil rights record that still prevailed. As more people began to wrestle with the discrepancy between the ideals touted in the Declaration of Independence and Constitution and the reality of life in the U.S. for minority groups, including African-Americans, it became more and more evident that something had to change. People began to speak out, and as they did, tension mounted as U.S. culture grappled with this inconsistency between the ideal and the real.

It was in this environment of growing tension that one woman decided she had had enough. With a simple, non-violent—even polite—act of defiance, Rosa Parks, a 42-year-old seamstress, would spark a movement that would ultimately change the face of a nation. On December 1, 1955, Parks boarded the Cleveland Avenue bus in Montgomery, Alabama. Segregation laws at the time had designated a black and white area of the bus, and Parks sat in the first row in the black section. As the bus filled up, all of the seats in the white section were occupied, and when white passengers were forced to stand, the bus driver asked Parks, along with three other passengers in that first row of the black section, to surrender their seats so that the white passengers could sit.

The three others asked to resign their seats did so, but Parks refused to move when asked by the bus driver, James F. Blake, to vacate her seat for the white passengers. She later said she thought of Emmett Till, an African-American teenager who was lynched in Mississippi after reportedly flirting with a white woman, and she just couldn't bring herself to move. Parks had had enough of being treated like a second-class citizen. Blake informed her he would call the police and have her arrested, and she told him that he should do just that. Parks was bailed out of jail that evening, but her case sparked the Montgomery bus boycott, where some 40,000 African-Americans boycotted riding the bus in Montgomery on the day of her trial, December 5, 1955.

The group that initially organized the boycott recognized their success and realized that they needed to form a new organization if they wanted to continue the protest. The new group was dubbed the Montgomery Improvement Association, and a young, mostly unknown minister was elected as president of what became known as the MIA. That minister was the Reverend Martin Luther King, Jr. of the Dexter Avenue Baptist Church. King later wrote in his book, *Stride Toward Freedom*, that Parks' arrest was the catalyst for the protests to follow, but that the ultimate cause was the long history of injustices that had occurred since Africans were first forcibly brought to the American colonies. He expressed the essence of that sentiment when he wrote, "Actually, no one can understand the action of Mrs. Parks unless he realizes that eventually the cup of endurance runs over, and the human personality cries out, 'I can take it no longer.'"

In a simple act of defiance, a quiet, mature woman ignited a fire in the soul of a nation. That fire still burns even as a single person struggles for their equality in a country that touted the God-given equality of all men while, at the same time, building its economy on the backs of slaves. Parks' refusal to give up her seat raised awareness and inspired others to act. She wrote of her action that, "I would like to be remembered as a person who wanted to be free... so other people would be also free." As a hero of the civil rights movement, she has achieved that goal and so much more. Her actions set an example that still has relevance today as a divided nation continues to struggle with questions of inequality in an increasingly complicated world.

Chapter One
A Dark Legacy

"It is impossible to struggle for civil rights, equal rights for blacks, without including whites. Because equal rights, fair play, justice, are all like the air: we all have it, or none of us has it. That is the truth of it."

—Maya Angelou

In the immediate aftermath of the Civil War, a period known as the Reconstruction Era (1865-1877), there were three visions associated with how the recovery from the war would proceed. One, referred to as the reconciliationist vision, was rooted in helping to cope with the devastation the war had brought. The destruction was significant as the war had resulted in more American casualties than both World War I and World War II combined would in the future. Additionally, family members on opposing sides of the war were forced to fight against one another, something which created profound and painful divisions. The second post-war vision, known as the white supremacist vision, was focused on terror and violence aimed at re-establishing at least the ideals of the Confederacy. The third one, known as the emancipationist vision, was focused on achieving full freedom, including citizenship and constitutional equality, for African-Americans.

As an end to the war grew near, President Lincoln set up reconstructed governments in those states that were under the control of the Union army. These included Tennessee, Arkansas, and Louisiana. He also experimented in establishing equality for African-Americans by giving newly freed slaves land, but both he and his successor, Andrew Johnson, took moderate positions on bringing the southern states back to normal. Johnson, in fact, followed a lenient policy with regard to ex-Confederate soldiers by placing them in power, and he was opposed to the enfranchisement of all freedmen (freed slaves), which Lincoln supported.

After Lincoln's assassination, Johnson was able to enact his vision of how to get the southern states back to normal until a Republican coalition came to power in 1866. They removed the former Confederate soldiers Johnson had put into power and began the process of transforming southern society by establishing a free labor economy and protecting the legal rights of freedmen. They created the U.S. Army and Freedmen's Bureau to act in this regard. The Bureau negotiated labor contracts for freedmen and set up schools and churches. Frustrated by Johnson's opposition to their efforts, the so-called Radical Republicans behind this progressive vision even filed impeachment charges against the president in 1866, but the action failed, though notably only by one vote.

The U.S. Congress then passed two bills aimed at protecting recently freed slaves and helping them achieve equality. The first bill extended the life of the U.S. Army and Freedmen's Bureau, which had originally been formed as a temporary organization to assist refugees and freed slaves in the immediate aftermath of the Civil War. The second bill defined all persons born in the United States, including African-Americans, as citizens with all the rights as described in the Constitution. President Johnson vetoed these two bills, and that act permanently ruptured his relationship with Congress, something which would have lasting consequences. Congress voted to override his veto, which was the first time a bill became law in this way, and they would later vote to impeach Johnson in 1868. However, despite the vote to impeach him, the Senate would not get the two-thirds majority vote needed to convict him and remove him from office. They once again fell short by one vote, though it represented the first impeachment of an incumbent president in United States history.

The next president, Ulysses S. Grant, supported the Radicals and their reconstruction efforts. He took office on March 4, 1869, and remained so until March 4, 1877. He vigorously enforced the protection of African-Americans in the south, and he used the Enforcement Act passed by Congress to effectively wipe out the first incarnation of the Ku Klux Klan. The Klan, as it was known, was initially founded by six former Confederate officers sometime between December of 1865 and August of 1866. It started as a fraternal social club, but in 1867, there was a gradual transformation into an organization that believed it had a serious purpose. That mission was rooted in white supremacy, and the Klan soon became a vigilante group dedicated to restoring white supremacy through threats and violence, including murder, against African-Americans and the white Republicans who had fought and continued to fight for their equality.

The Klan would be somewhat successful in weakening the black political establishment by assassinating and threatening those who were in or were seeking public office. Their methods, however, undermined their efforts insofar as the backlash created resulted in the passage of federal laws that restored order and the morale of southern Republicans. Those laws also helped enable African-Americans to exercise their constitutional rights. Many historians, as a result, argue the first version of the Klan was a political failure, to that extent as achieving their goals was concerned, and that fact subsequently allowed the group to be effectively suppressed by President Grant's efforts. It wouldn't be until 1915 that the Klan would be reconstituted.

Grant, for his part, while successful in his efforts against the Klan, was never able to resolve the growing tension between two factions within the Republican party—the northern Republicans versus those from southern states, who became known as Scalawags by forces in the south opposing Reconstruction. Part of the northern effort had included coalitions of southern freedmen and recent black and white arrivals from the north, who became known as carpetbaggers. The northern faction worked with cooperative southern Republicans to form biracial state governments, and they introduced various reconstruction programs including such projects as funding public schools, establishing charitable institutions, and offering massive aid for improving railroad transportation and shipping.

There was strong resistance to these efforts, and while Grant was able to suppress the Klan, white Democrats, known as Redeemers, slowly began to regain control state by state. They were even able to make major gains in the north after the Panic of 1873 led to a deep economic depression as well as the collapse of many of the railroad improvement efforts ongoing in the southern states at the time. This marks the point at which the Reconstruction Era began to wind down. It was a staggered process, ending at different times in different states, but the Compromise of 1877 ceased all military intervention in southern politics. As a result, Republican political control in the south collapsed.

The next period in history was labeled by the white southerners as Redemption. During this time, white-dominated legislatures enacted Jim Crow laws, which enforced racial segregation. The phrase Jim Crow originated with a song-and-dance character known as Jump Jim Crow. The song-and-dance was a caricature of African-Americans, and it was performed by the white actor Thomas D. Rice in blackface. The act first surfaced in 1832, and as a result of Rice's fame, Jim Crow became a pejorative term for "Negro." Thus, the statutes passed by the southern states as a means of institutionalizing racism became known as Jim Crow laws. These laws effectively disenfranchised most African-Americans and many poor white people as well, and the legislators imposed the white supremacy vision of Reconstruction throughout the south. This time period also became known as the age of Jim Crow.

In 1883, the United States Supreme Court ruled that the Civil Rights Act passed in 1875 was unconstitutional. The act had forbidden discrimination on the basis of race by hotels, trains, and in other public spaces. The court's decision effectively limited the rights of African-Americans, and it strengthened the Jim Crow laws. Furthermore, another decision by the Supreme Court, in the case of Plessy v. Ferguson, affirmed the concept of separate but equal used by legislatures to legalize segregation and discrimination not just against African-Americans, but against Asian-Americans, Irish-Americans, and other immigrant groups as well.

This allowed lawmakers to enact numerous laws restricting these groups in public life, segregating them in schools and other facilities, legalizing employment and housing discrimination, banning interracial marriage, and setting limitations on property ownership. Additionally, non-immigrant Native Americans also faced the rising tide of discrimination as they fought against further expansion into their territories and broken treaty obligations. Women, too, were fighting for their own rights as they sought the right to vote. The decision in the court outraged many in the black—and white—community. Henry McNeal Turner, the 12th elected minister of the African Methodist Episcopal Church and a former politician in the Georgia legislature, denounced the decision, stating, "The world has never witnessed such barbarous laws entailed upon a free people as have grown out of the decision of the United States Supreme Court, issued October 15, 1883." The decision would indeed have a lasting, negative effect on the effort to secure civil rights for all U.S. citizens.

Chapter Two

The Winds of Change

"The greatest movement for social justice our country has ever known is the civil rights movement and it was totally rooted in a love ethic."

—bell hooks

In United States history, the end of the nineteenth century was a time of change. Urbanization and industrialization were bringing about dramatic population shifts, as were immigration, the expansion of education, and the settlement of the West. There was more diversity than ever before, and as has been seen in other contexts, that diversity combined with economic challenges often resulted in struggles over who has the right to various resources. People fear they won't have enough, and they seek to limit access so they can ensure their own abundance. Of course, they often justify the imposition of limitations by placing blame on those whose access they would restrict. Or, they argue in the name of a higher cause, usually God or country.

Such was the case at the end of the nineteenth century when the U.S. Supreme Court limited the rights of numerous groups including African-Americans by declaring the Civil Rights Act of 1875 unconstitutional. It opened the door for the passage of more Jim Crow laws that would institutionalize racism for years to come, and it justified the discriminatory laws that already existed.

During the immediate aftermath of the Civil War, African-Americans made numerous advances toward the goal of establishing their equality. Senator Hiram Revels of Mississippi and Representative Joseph Rainey of South Carolina arrived in Congress in 1870. Their arrival represented significant progress as just a decade earlier, those seats were held by slave owners. On February 3, 1870, the 15th Amendment giving African-American men the right to vote was ratified, and Senator Revels was often introduced as, the "Fifteenth Amendment in flesh and blood." Less than two decades later, by 1887, there were no African-Americans in Congress. It heralded in a period when Congress would diminish any focus on racial equality as southern conservatives significantly increased their political power.

In the years after 1890, nearly all the political advances made by African-Americans in the Reconstruction Era would be rolled back and/or eradicated. In fact, in southern states, African-Americans were more systematically and rigidly segregated than they had been during slavery. As C. Vann Woodward writes, the Jim Crow laws instituted in the post-reconstruction time period "did not assign the subordinate group a fixed status in society. They were constantly pushing the Negro farther down."

During this time period, there were also major shifts occurring in the political realm beyond the question of racial equality. The Republican Party, which was the party of Lincoln, and whose members had supported, even radically so, the ideal of racial equality, had found themselves out of power and out of favor in the south. The party split into two factions, one of which clung to the traditional ideals while the other part argued that the only way for Republicans to regain power in the south was to abandon the freedmen and deprioritize racial politics. That combined with rapid industrialization, which was bringing numerous economic and social changes, resulted in the displacement of race reform on the political agenda.

The dramatic changes occurring in the United States at the end of the nineteenth century created a level of cultural uncertainty that resulted in what historian Robert Wiebe described as widespread "dislocation and bewilderment." As a consequence of all of the rapid changes, the Republican Party recast itself around commercial interests rather than their previous focus on racial politics. The strategy worked, bringing the party success in the 1890s. Meanwhile, black constituencies in the south were disappearing rapidly. Many states rewrote their constitutions and created a number of electoral devices designed to limit African-American participation in the political process. These included poll taxes that were prohibitively expensive for most blacks and many whites, voter registration laws that required documents many voters, particularly African-Americans, did not possess, and educational tests, administered and graded by white registrars, that many African-Americans did not have the education to pass. These strategies worked, allowing the Democratic Party to continue to dominate southern politics. Moreover, the change in focus to commercial issues and foreign policy on the part of the Republican Party, also known as the Grand Old Party (GOP), meant that the racist policies enacted by the Democrats faced little opposition.

Though there were black legislators elected to Congress during this time, they weren't elected in enough numbers to have any significant influence over the policies enacted, and the white supremacists who held power utilized numerous devices to disenfranchise the black vote. This included gerrymandering—or redrawing the boundaries of congressional districts—to restrict the election of African-Americans to office or to minimize their power if elected.

The boundaries of voting districts were often drawn in a convoluted manner in order to break up the black population of the area so that whites outnumbered black voters in the newly established districts, or with a view to consolidating the black vote into one district, which would minimize the influence of any politicians elected by that district. The latter process was known as "packing," while attempts to scatter African-American voters amidst white voting populations was called "cracking." One area in South Carolina was so winding and narrow; it was dubbed the shoestring district while another section in North Carolina was roughly the shape of a salamander. Gerrymandering is still utilized in modern U.S. politics to shape the electorate, and it remains the subject of considerable debate.

By the end of the nineteenth century, the Jim Crow laws along with a series of Supreme Court rulings had eroded any legal basis for equality. In the *Plessy v. Ferguson* case of 1896, the court upheld a Louisiana law that required the provision of separate but equal accommodations for blacks and whites. The decision effectively sanctioned segregation. Another court case in 1898, *Williams v. Mississippi*, endorsed laws that prevented black men from serving on juries. *Giles v. Harris*, in 1903, upheld the grandfather clause, which was a legal mechanism passed by seven southern states to deny suffrage to African-Americans. Even if they met the strict voting requirements that these states had adopted, those African-Americans who were allowed to vote prior to 1867, and their lineal descendants, were now prevented from voting. The grandfather clause was one of the chief disenfranchising mechanisms used at southern constitutional conventions during this time.

By the turn of the twentieth century, African-American civil rights had suffered major declines. The beginning of the twentieth century heralded in the Age of Progressivism, which sought to bring about significant social reform through professionalization and standardization. The focus of progressives also included political reforms such as direct primary elections, popular elections of senators, and women's suffrage. The focus on professionalization and the need for expertise, however, meant that many of the progressive efforts often complemented Jim Crow, because it sought to limit voting to those who were considered qualified. The rationalization for this was rooted in social Darwinism, which postulated that social success was the result of superior biological traits, an evolutionary concept grossly distorted and misapplied to a social context in order to suit racist ideology.

For their part, African-Americans participated as much as possible given their marginalized position. In 1909, the National Association for the Advancement of Colored People (NAACP) was founded, and African-American soldiers made significant contributions in both World War I and World War II. The 1920s brought the flowering of African-American intellectualism and artistic talent with the Harlem Renaissance. Given the repressive system in the southern U.S., many blacks migrated to northern cities. This demographic shift would significantly influence events into the future.

Politically, the major party positions began to change. At the turn of the century, both sides were trying to win the west. The Republicans had already moved from racial politics to a focus on commerce and foreign policy in the attempt to gain support in southern states. In the early twentieth century, a prominent Democrat, William Jennings Bryan, began to argue that the government should ensure social justice through the expansion of federal powers. This had previously been the Republican Party's platform, but the use of it by the Republicans had been favorable to big business interests at the expense of "the little guy." The Democrats then began to promise the same big government benefits to the so-called little guys, many of whom had gone west.

By the time Franklin D. Roosevelt won re-election in 1936 on the strength of the Great Depression remedying program known as the New Deal, the parties had effectively switched platforms. With an emphasis on social justice, the Democratic Party began to adopt increasingly progressive, liberal ideals which formed the basis for their modern-day platform. The Republican Party continued to emphasize a platform that favored commercial interests, and increasingly, small government. That continues to be their platform in the modern era.

Though the major political parties had changed their ideologies, little changed with regard to racial politics. The NAACP, however, was becoming increasingly active in the political realm. They began to focus their efforts on getting anti-lynching legislation passed. Over 1,200 blacks were lynched in the south between 1901 and 1929. In the 1920s, the NAACP became a significant political force under the leadership of James Weldon Johnson. Johnson lobbied friendly legislators who introduced several versions of bills attempting to outlaw lynching. Though none were passed, the intense pressure levied by the NAACP in combination with their public awareness campaign is generally seen to have led to a reduction in lynching after the 1920s.

In 1928, Oscar De Priest of Illinois became the first African-American to serve in Congress since 1901. His victory renewed hope in the African-American community that they would once again gain influence in national politics. However, with only a dozen more African-Americans elected over the next 30 years, the journey toward achieving representation was tedious. Segregation remained in place, and African-American Congressmen, like their black constituents, were subjected to racial slurs and prejudicial slights. Still, the momentum for change was growing. The progress was slow but steady. It was expressed by New York Congressman, Representative Adam Clayton Powell, Jr.—who became a symbol of political activism for millions of African-Americans—when he said, "Keep the faith, baby, spread it gently and walk together, children." His actions in Congress helped lay the groundwork for the political activism of the 1960s.

Chapter Three

The Stage Is Set

"As far back as I can remember, I knew there was something wrong with our way of life when people could be mistreated because of the color of their skin."

—Rosa Parks

By 1955, racism was rampant in the United States. Segregation based on the concept of separate but equal remained the official policy. Violence against African-Americans was common and often legally sanctioned. African-American communities were oppressed and were kept in poverty by unequal access to services, including education. Though the official policy was separate but equal, the reality was that the services available to African-Americans were vastly inferior to those offered to European-Americans. The same was also true for other minority groups. This was the context in which Rosa Parks defiantly refused to give up her seat on the bus, an act which sparked a cultural revolution. But, who was Rosa Parks?

Rosa Parks was born Rosa Louise McCauley on February 4, 1913, in Tuskegee, Alabama. Her parents were Leona and James McCauley. James was a carpenter. When her parents separated, she moved with her mother to Pine

Level, Alabama where they lived with her maternal grandparents. She attended rural school and had begun a secondary education at the Alabama State Teachers College for Negroes, but she had to drop out of that to care for her ailing mother and grandmother.

As was common for many African-Americans, she was exposed to racism at an early age. School buses took white students to school in Pine Level, but black students had to walk. Parks cited this fact as being one of the first ways in which she came to realize there was a black world and a white world. She was also repeatedly bullied by white children in her neighborhood. The Ku Klux Klan, which had reappeared on the social scene in 1915, had become an active, well-organized, white supremacy group in the south. By 1921, it had adopted a national and state structure based on a modern business model that used paid recruiters to appeal to new members. At its peak in the mid-1920s, it included approximately 15% of the nation's eligible population or about 4-5 million men. As a young girl, Parks remembered seeing the Klan march past their house, and she recalled her grandfather guarding the door with a shotgun.

In 1932, at age 19, Rosa married a barber from Montgomery, Alabama named Raymond Parks. He was an active member of the NAACP, and it was at his urging that Rosa finished her high school education in 1933. At that time, less than 7% of African-Americans had a high school diploma. Rosa also managed to register to vote despite the discriminatory Jim Crow laws in place in Alabama. Her husband's involvement in the NAACP exposed her to more of the injustices perpetrated against African-Americans. When she married him, the NAACP was active in collecting money for the defense of the Scottsboro Boys, who were a group of black men falsely accused of raping two white women. By 1943, Rosa herself became active in the civil rights movement.

Parks joined the Montgomery chapter of the NAACP and was elected secretary. She was the only woman in the organization at the time. The leader, Edgar Nixon, believed that women should stay in the kitchen, but conceded that he needed a secretary and Parks was a good one. In 1944, Parks investigated the gang rape of Recy Taylor. Taylor was a black woman from Abbeville, Alabama, who had been kidnapped and brutally raped by six white men. No charges were ever brought against the perpetrators, but her case prompted action by civil rights activists, who along with Parks, formed the Committee for Equal Justice for Mrs. Recy Taylor. It was considered one of the strongest campaigns of its kind.

Soon after 1944, Parks briefly worked at Maxwell Air Force Base, which, because it was federal property, did not allow racial segregation. Parks was able to ride on an integrated trolley, and she later told her biographer that this experience really opened her eyes. Additionally, in the 1940s, Parks and her husband were members of the Voters' League, which was active in helping black citizens pass the educational tests required for voter registration.

Rosa Parks later worked for a politically liberal white couple, Clifford and Virginia Durr, who sponsored her to attend the Highlander Folk School in the summer of 1955, which was an education center for activists in workers' rights and racial equality. At the school, her mentor was veteran organizer Septima Clark, who would later be referred to as the "Queen Mother" of the civil rights movement. At a time when education for both African-Americans and women was limited, she earned a Master's degree and would later establish "Citizenship Schools" to teach reading and citizenship rights to adults throughout the deep south as a means of empowering the African-American community.

In August of 1955, Emmett Till, a black teenager visiting relatives in Mississippi, was brutally murdered after it was claimed that he flirted with a young white woman. Till was lynched, and his death inflamed civil rights activists. He later became an icon of the civil rights movement. On November 27 that same year, Rosa Parks attended a meeting at the Dexter Avenue Baptist Church in Montgomery, Alabama. The meeting was organized to discuss the Till case as well as two other murders, those of George W. Lee and Lamar Smith, both of whom were civil rights activists and both of whom were killed in Mississippi. Parks was particularly saddened and disturbed when the invited speaker, T.R.M. Howard, broke the news of the acquittal of the two men who lynched Emmett Till.

This was the context in which Rosa Parks would, within 5 days, board a bus and commit a non-violent act of civil disobedience. She would refuse to relinquish her bus seat to white passengers, a small act that would bring remarkable changes in a country sitting on top of a powder keg of rising racial tension. Parks' arrest was the spark that lit the fuse, the proverbial final straw that broke the camel's back. The confluence of events that brought Rosa Parks to the point where she found she could no longer comply with the racist policies of Jim Crow had also brought the African-American community to the point where the "cup of endurance," as King later dubbed it, was full. The horrific injustices perpetrated on the African-American community since the earliest days of slavery provided the fuel for the raging fire that would be ignited by a comparatively minor injustice. Parks was not beaten, raped, nor lynched because of her act of defiance; she was merely arrested, but this relatively small crime committed against this mild-mannered woman was the drop that finally made King's "cup of endurance" run over. The African-American community could take it no longer, the dam was broken, and a flood that carried with it over 100 years of unthinkable discrimination was raging toward white culture in America.

Chapter Four

The Civil Rights Movement

"There is just so much hurt, disappointment, and oppression one can take. . . . The line between reason and madness grows thinner."

—Rosa Parks

During World War II, U.S. soldiers had proudly fought against the evil they saw in Adolf Hitler. Few who would be witness to the horrors perpetrated by the hatred born of prejudice would deny that those who committed such atrocities were evil. Upon returning home, however, a proud nation, which perceived of its role in the war as just and heroic, began to grapple with the inconsistencies of its own prejudicial policies.

Women, who had aided in the war effort, both as military personnel and civilians, had played a substantial role in American success. Minority soldiers had also made inestimable contributions, without which the U.S. military would have been significantly hampered in the war effort. These impressive contributions included such notable involvement as that made by the Navajo code talkers, whose codes the enemies were never able to decipher, and the Tuskegee Airmen, whose bravery and success in defending bombers against enemy attack was so well-recognized that even openly racist, white bomber pilots requested them as their escorts into enemy territory.

Upon returning home following the war, however, women and minorities were expected to go back to the life they had known before the war. Women were supposed to leave the jobs where they had felt valued and return to the kitchen, while minorities were required to go back to a life of subjugation after fighting against it on the global stage alongside their white comrades in arms. The proverbial genie, however, was out of the bottle and there was no going back. African-Americans were beginning to make strides toward more equality, and as a result, they were starting to demand more of it.

By the spring of 1941, as America was gearing up for war, President Roosevelt had issued an executive order banning discrimination in the defense industries. He did so to prevent race riots as black labor leaders threatened to march on Washington to ensure they would be hired equally for jobs in those sectors. During the war, the NAACP, along with other civil rights organizations, worked tirelessly to end discrimination in the armed forces. On the home front, the Congress of Racial Equality (CORE) was founded to challenge Jim Crow laws in the south. After the war, President Truman appointed a select committee to investigate racial conditions. Truman later abolished racial discrimination in the military. The NAACP also won significant Supreme Court victories during this time. Additionally, African-Americans achieved several notable firsts, including in major league baseball where Jackie Robinson broke the color barrier. Civil rights activists also began to press their case more forcefully. Bayard Rustin and George Houser led black and white riders on what they called a "Journey of Reconciliation" to protest racial segregation on interstate buses.

The laws of racial segregation on buses were in place as early as 1900 when Montgomery, Alabama had passed an ordinance empowering conductors to segregate bus passengers by race. That law had stated that passengers would not be required to give up their seats if the bus was crowded and no seats were available, even though the driver could assign seats by race. The custom, however, quickly became one of asking black riders to move when there were no more seats for white passengers. Generally, the so-called colored section of the bus was in the rear, and these were limited even though African-Americans made up some 75% of the ridership. Additionally, if white riders were already on the bus and a black passenger wanted to ride, they would have to board at the front to pay the driver, then disembark and re-enter the bus through the rear door so they wouldn't pass by the white passengers. The same bus driver, James F. Blake, who asked Rosa Parks to give up her seat had also driven off without her on one previous occasion when she had had to do just that. Parks was determined never to ride his bus again after that, but when she entered the bus on December 1, 1955, she didn't realize it was the same driver.

Parks had been working all day when she boarded the Cleveland Avenue bus belonging to the Montgomery City Lines around 6 p.m. It has been erroneously reported that she refused to give up her seat that evening because she was physically tired after a long day of work. Parks disputes this, asserting that she was simply emotionally tired of being treated in such a disrespectful manner. Parks was seated in the colored section near the middle of the bus with three other African-Americans. When the bus filled up, and white passengers had to stand, the driver moved the colored section sign back behind the row where Parks and her fellow passengers were seated. At first, none of them moved when asked to surrender their seats, but as the driver became more insistent, the other three individuals moved. Parks stated that "When that white driver stepped back toward us, when he waved his hand and ordered us up and out of our seats, I felt a determination to cover my body like a quilt on a winter night." She also said that she thought of Emmett Till and she just couldn't do what the driver was asking.

Parks recounted that when Blake asked her why she wouldn't move, she answered that she didn't think she should have to stand up. He then told her he would call the police, and she said, "You may do that." Parks later told Sydney Rogers during a radio interview that "I would have to know for once and for all what rights I had as a human being and a citizen." Parks was charged with violating Chapter 6, Section 11 of the Montgomery City penal code. Edgar Nixon, who was the president of the Montgomery chapter of the NAACP and leader of the

Pullman Porters Union, bailed her out of jail that evening. He was accompanied by her friend, Clifford Durr, a white Alabama lawyer who made his career defending activists and others accused of disloyalty, including those charged with disloyalty to the United States during the McCarthy era.

After Parks had been bailed out of jail, Nixon consulted Jo Ann Robinson, a member of the Women's Political Council and an Alabama State College professor. They both believed that Parks' case presented an excellent opportunity to organize civil rights action. Parks was a mature, quiet, married, well-respected African-American citizen, who though active in the civil rights movement, had not been in trouble before. Thus, veteran activists believed her case would resonate even beyond the African-American community. The result of their meeting was the Montgomery Bus Boycott, which was the epitome of a grassroots organization movement.

Robinson had stayed up all night copying 35,000 handbills announcing the boycott, which was endorsed by the Women's Political Council. On Sunday, December 4, 1955, the day before Parks' trial, the boycott was announced in black churches throughout the area. Additionally, an article on the front page of the Montgomery Advertiser helped to spread the word. The goal was to continue the boycott until everyone was treated with the same level of courtesy, black drivers were hired by the company, and seating in the middle of the bus was handled on a first-come, first-served basis.

On December 5, 1955, Parks was tried for disorderly conduct and violation of a local ordinance. She was found guilty and fined $10, but she immediately appealed her conviction and challenged the legality of racial segregation. Though it rained that day, some 40,000 African-Americans boycotted riding the bus. Some were able to ride in carpools, some used cabs operated by black owners who had agreed to charge the same fare as the bus (10 cents), and the remainder of the commuters walked, some as far as 20 miles. Parks was overwhelmed by the effort. When she was greeted with a standing ovation at a meeting of leaders to discuss strategy and asked to speak that same evening, she stated simply, "Why, you've said enough."

The group who met that evening, however, realized they would need to do more if they hoped to continue the boycott until their demands for equality and simple courtesy were met. They decided to form a new organization dedicated to that effort. It was called the Montgomery Improvement Association (MIA), and the group elected a relatively unknown minister as president. That minister was the Reverend Martin Luther King, Jr., who was the minister of the Dexter Avenue Baptist Church. Under King's leadership, black citizens would continue the boycott for 381 days, causing dozens of buses to stand idle for months and severely damaging the transit company's finances.

The boycott ended when the city repealed the law requiring segregation on public buses after the U.S. Supreme Court ruled it was unconstitutional in the

Browder v. Gayle ruling. This case involved four women who had been discriminated against by bus drivers, at least one of whom, Claudette Colvin, had been arrested before Parks. Colvin was a 15-year-old girl and was the first person to be arrested for refusing to give up her bus seat in Montgomery. She was arrested nine months before Parks. The other plaintiffs in the case were Aurelia Browder, Susie McDonald, and Mary Louise Smith. There had been a fifth woman, Jeanetta Reese, but she dropped out after being intimidated by people in the white community. Their federal civil action lawsuit was filed against the mayor of Montgomery, W.A. Gayle, and while Parks was considered an ideal plaintiff, Durr, who filed this lawsuit, worried that an appeal of her case would get bogged down in the Alabama state courts. That's why he decided it was better to proceed with the others. With the victory of this case in the U.S. Supreme Court, buses were desegregated, and the boycott ended.

As for Parks' case, the Alabama appellate court ruled that, because her attorney failed to make assignments of error, there was nothing for the court to review, and it, therefore, upheld her conviction. The incident, however, made her an icon of the Civil Rights Movement, which because of her courage, was gathering steam. Parks, herself, would continue to play an important role in the movement as her life was forever changed by one small act of defiance.

Chapter Five

Life after the Boycott

"I have learned over the years that when one's mind is made up, this diminishes fear; knowing what must be done does away with fear."

—Rosa Parks

After her arrest, Rosa Parks lost her department store job because of economic sanctions that were commonly used against activists. She was unable to find another job, and she also found herself disagreeing with the leaders of the Montgomery civil rights movement, including Dr. King, about how the movement should proceed. In 1957, she and her husband decided to move to Hampton, Virginia. There, she was able to get a job as a hostess in an inn at a historically black college, the Hampton Institute. She, her husband, and her mother decided to move again, later that same year, to Detroit. There, she became increasingly involved in fighting discrimination, particularly in the housing industry.

Upon moving to Detroit, Parks had encountered several signs of discrimination in numerous sectors of the city. Schools remained segregated, services to black neighborhoods were substandard, and there was also housing segregation. Parks was somewhat surprised, having believed that things in the north, particularly in larger cities, would be different. She began participating in the movements for open and fair housing. As part of her civil rights work in Detroit, she gave vital assistance to the congressional campaign of John Conyers. It was his first campaign, and thanks to Parks, his profile was significantly elevated after she convinced Martin Luther King to endorse him. He was elected, and shortly thereafter, hired Parks as a receptionist for his office in Detroit. She would work in that position until her retirement in 1988. Conyers said of Parks, "You treated her with deference because she was so quiet, so serene—just a very special person . . . There was only one Rosa Parks."

In her position as Conyers' receptionist, Parks was able to participate in activism at the national level. She participated in the Selma to Montgomery marches, the Freedom Now Party, and the Lowndes County Freedom Organization, and she also befriended her personal hero, Malcolm X. Additionally, she lived just a mile from the center of the 1967 Detroit riots, which she considered to have been provoked by housing discrimination that had resulted in the displacement of 43,096 people, 70% of whom were black. She collaborated with several groups investigating police abuse in the aftermath of those riots and worked to help rebuild the area as well. Among her other notable contributions are that she attended the Philadelphia Black Power Conference, the Black Political Convention, and she supported and visited the Black Panther school in Oakland.

In the 1970s, Parks organized support for gaining the freedom of people considered to be political prisoners in the United States. She also helped found the Detroit chapter of the Joann Little Defense Committee, which supported a woman's right to defend herself from rape, even if that meant killing someone as a result. The support of Joann Little resulted in her acquittal for murdering a prison guard who was attempting to sexually assault her. Her acquittal was a victory for both women and African-Americans. Parks also found the time to book almost constant speaking engagements. After the deaths of her husband, from throat cancer, and her brother, also from cancer, Parks became removed from the civil rights movement in the late 1970s. She also suffered two broken bones when she fell on an icy sidewalk, and after this, she decided to move with her mother into an apartment for senior citizens, where she would nurse her mother through cancer and dementia. Her mother, Leona, died in 1979 at age 92.

The 1970s had been a decade of change and loss for Parks, who was, at the beginning of 1980, widowed and without immediate family. She decided to rededicate herself to the civil rights movement. She started by co-founding the Rosa L. Parks Scholarship Foundation, and it was to this foundation that she donated the majority of her speaking fees. She also co-founded the Rosa and Raymond Parks Institute for Self Development, which runs what are called "Pathways to Freedom" bus tours to introduce young people to civil rights issues. The buses visit Underground Railroad sites throughout the United

States. Parks was also active in women's rights. She served on the Board of Advocates of Planned Parenthood.

In the 1990s, Parks published two books. One, *Rosa Parks: My Story*, published in 1992, was an autobiography aimed at younger readers, and the other, *Quiet Strength*, published in 1995, was her memoir, which focused on her faith. After being attacked and beaten in her home in central Detroit, the 81-year-old Parks moved into the Riverfront Towers, a high-rise apartment building owned by Little Caesar's owner Mike Ilitch, who offered to pay her housing expenses for as long as was necessary. By 2002, Parks was in failing physical and mental health and was unable to manage her financial affairs. She reportedly received an eviction notice when she neglected to pay her $1800 per month rent. After her cause was taken up by the Hartford Memorial Baptist Church in Detroit, and her case subsequently became highly publicized in 2004, the executives of the ownership company forgave all back rent and announced that she could live there, rent-free, for the remainder of her life. She was 91 years old at the time. Elaine Steele, the manager of the non-profit Rosa and Raymond Parks Institute, later claimed the eviction notices were sent in error, but her heirs and interest organizations claimed her affairs had been mismanaged.

Rosa Parks, Mother of the U.S. Civil Rights Movement, died of natural causes on October 24, 2005. She was 92 years old. On October 27, 2005, city officials of Montgomery, Alabama, and Detroit, Michigan reserved the front seats of their city buses with black ribbons in her honor until her funeral. Parks' body was flown to

Montgomery and taken in a horse-drawn hearse to the St. Paul African Methodist Episcopal church, where she lay in repose until the next day. Her body was then transported to Washington, DC where she became the first woman and the second African-American to lie in state in the Capitol. She was the first American who had not been a government official to do so. Her body was then returned to Detroit. There, she lay in repose at the Charles H. Wright Museum of African American History until her funeral service on November 2, at the Greater Grace Temple Church in Detroit. The Michigan National Guard laid the American flag over her casket and carried it to a horse-drawn hearse. She was interred at Detroit's Woodlawn Cemetery in the chapel's mausoleum, and the chapel was renamed the Rosa L. Parks Freedom Chapel in her honor. She had already purchased and placed her headstone on the location she selected. It reads, "Rosa L. Parks, wife, 1913-2005." The long struggle of this quiet, dignified woman who gave rise to a movement that changed a nation was finally over, and she could rest at last after a life well-done.

The movement her quiet act of defiance sparked had made many sizeable achievements over the years, much of which was helped along by Parks' involvement. Though the 15th Amendment had granted African-American males the right to vote, the restrictive Jim Crow laws had allowed states to institute discriminatory practices such as literacy tests and poll taxes that targeted mainly African-Americans and other poor minority communities. The Voting Rights Act of 1965 eliminated many of those policies. The Civil Rights Act of 1968 ended housing and school segregation. President John F. Kennedy had banned discriminatory hiring practices by government contractors by use of executive order in 1961. His successor, Lyndon B. Johnson, banned employment discrimination for any organization receiving federal contracts and subcontracts, again by executive order, in 1965. These executive orders were cited as the basis for affirmative action policies adopted by universities seeking to ensure equality in the admission process. Today, discrimination for reasons of race is illegal in virtually every context—housing, employment, and public services.

The fight for equality continues, however, as the movement has also suffered many disappointments. The third incarnation of the Ku Klux Klan occurred in the 1950s and 1960s as the civil rights movement was gaining more ground. The second incarnation, which had peaked at a membership of 4-5 million men in the 1920s had largely collapsed when that membership dropped to 30,000 in 1930. In the 50s and 60s, it resurfaced, and this time the group formed alliances with southern police departments. While much of the accomplishments made by civil rights activists ultimately caused the Klan to go underground, the group was responsible for much of the violence against African-Americans, particularly in the south, during this volatile time in history. Notably, members of the Klan were convicted of the killing of children in the bombing of the 16th Street Baptist Church in Birmingham, Alabama in 1963, and murder in the deaths of civil rights workers in Mississippi in 1964.

Today, they are considered as a subversive or terrorist organization, and their membership is only estimated at somewhere around 5,000; however, there has been a recent resurgence of white supremacy groups as politics have taken a more nationalistic tone recently. The white supremacist groups do not call themselves the Ku Klux Klan, but they hold many of the same beliefs.

Martin Luther King, Jr. was assassinated on April 4, 1968, by James Earl Ray, who, though not known to be a Klan member, harbored significant prejudice against African-Americans and believed in segregation. Rosa Parks was once quoted as saying, "Well, you have to die sometime . . . then if they could kill me, I would just be dead." In his last speech, King had said about reaching the promised land of equality, "I might not get there with you." Both knew the risks they were taking, but they both also knew that with or without them, the movement would prevail. There have been numerous court challenges to laws that prohibit discrimination. There have also been, and continue to be, numerous attempts to undermine voting rights' protection and affirmative action. So far, most of these have ultimately failed, but those who would be subjected to oppression and all those who believe in equality, regardless of their race or gender, must remain vigilant against laws that would seek to undermine the advances made at such a high cost. As Edmund Burke so famously said, "The only thing necessary for the triumph of evil is for good men to do nothing."

Conclusion

Rosa Parks decided in December of 1955 that she had simply had enough. Accordingly, when she was asked, for no other reason than the color of her skin, to give up her seat for white passengers, in a non-violent act of defiance, she politely refused. She was subsequently arrested, and her arrest ignited a movement for people whose "cup of endurance" could contain no more injustice. And, so it was that an unknown minister, the Reverend Martin Luther King, Jr., was elected president of an organization created to continue the successful boycott of public transportation started to protest Parks' arrest. That boycott went on until the segregation on buses was ruled unconstitutional by the Supreme Court. It demonstrated the power of peaceful protest, a key component of King's strategy to gain equality for all African-Americans.

The movement did not begin with Parks. Many had made notable sacrifices and toiled tirelessly for justice before her, but there was something about that quiet, mature, dignified woman's polite refusal to comply with one more humiliating request born of a racist policy that struck a chord with the African-American community. It was perhaps serendipity—the right act, the right victim, at the right time. Leaders of the civil rights movement immediately recognized the significance of the response to the boycott initiated on Parks' behalf. Some 40,000 African-Americans responded to the request to boycott the buses even if it meant they walked as far as 20 miles to work. It was a tremendous statement from people who like Parks, had simply had enough.

From that moment, the movement only gained momentum, and it quickly began to resonate with the American people, even beyond the African-American community. Change was challenging and came at a high price. There were riots, murders, and bombings, but there was no turning back. World War II had shown the American citizenry the dark world of genocide to which prejudice and hatred could lead, and the ideals expressed in the Constitution and the Declaration of Independence were clearly at odds with a segregated society.

The heroism of American military personnel, including women and racial minorities, during World War II, could not be denied, making it harder to relegate those groups to a subordinate position in the post-war years. Furthermore, they were unwilling to accept that treatment after they, too, had seen the horrific results of a discriminatory ideology. As the American culture grappled with the discrepancy between the ideals that shaped the formation of its democracy and the reality of a segregated and distinctly separate but unequal society, tensions grew, and more people of all races began to speak out against the racist policies that had dominated to that point.

Many heroes emerged during this tumultuous time in American history, and there were many whose heroic actions were never fully recognized. Indeed, the women who had also refused to give up their seats on segregated buses and whose court case ultimately led to the Supreme

Court decision that declared the practice unconstitutional were never appropriately recognized for their contributions. There were also many who were lost in the violence that such foundational cultural change inevitably creates. Martin Luther King, Jr. was one of those. He, like Rosa Parks, recognized the peril that could come from their actions. Yet, they both continued to press their case, despite that danger. Their willingness to stay true to their cause, despite the personal danger it put them in, is a testament to the human spirit, and it is also a testament to what happens when one simply can take no more.

Parks hadn't intended to start a revolution that evening in Montgomery, Alabama. She was just unwilling, on a personal level, to accept any more unfair treatment. She was a dignified woman—not only a respected African-American woman—a well-respected woman in general. In her defiance, she was neither violent nor rude, and it was perhaps her quiet demeanor that generated the strong response by her community. She had done nothing to deserve the treatment she received. She wasn't a troublemaker, nor did she initiate the confrontation that occurred. No one could argue she had put herself in a position where she deserved what happened. She simply got on a bus, after a long day at work, to go home to her family. It is perhaps the mundane nature of the situation that generated the strong response.

Whatever the reason, the civil rights movement gained significant momentum from Parks' refusal to move that December day. She would continue to work for the rest of her life for the cause of equality, and she would continue to make significant contributions in that regard. Winston Churchill once said, "Courage is what it takes to stand up and speak; courage is also what it takes to sit down and listen." Given what Rosa Parks did, it also might be appropriate to add, courage is what it takes to stay seated, and change the world.

Printed in Great Britain
by Amazon